# This book belongs to:

_____

# It is a gift from:

_____

# WELCOME TO "MEET THE HORSES"

Get ready to color and discover the fascinating world of horses! Inside, you'll find fun coloring pages, along with interesting facts about horses, their behavior, and how they live. This book is not only a creative adventure but also a way to learn more about these incredible animals. Grab your crayons, explore the world of horses, and let your imagination run wild while you learn along the way!

## Fall in love with the horses.

# THEY EAT
## grass, hay and lucerne

THEY don't EAT:

MEAT

Horses cannot digest meat properly.

# HORSES
## are mammals and viviparous

*They drink milk from their mom.*

# Horses can give birth to TWINS

1

2

# HORSES
## REALLY FALL IN
## LOVE

# Horses

belong to the *Equidae family*, which also includes, donkeys and zebras.

# PONIES

Are a subtype of HORSE, distinguished by their smaller size, thicker manes, and sturdier build.

# HORSES ARE PART OF CHESS

Horses can run at an average speed of 25-30 mph during a sustained gallop, with the fastest reaching up to 55 mph over short distances.

THEY'RE SUPER FAST!

Horse shoes

# IT IS NOT IDEAL TO SHOE HORSES.

Horses with shoes are more prone to injuries like pulling a shoe, stepping on nails, or slipping on certain surfaces.

# Horses like to be brushed.

# hearing

Rotating ears detect distant sounds. A horse's hearing is about four times more acute than a human's.

# taste

**Prefers sweet, fresh foods.**

# Sight

Panoramic vision, but blind spots in front and behind.

# THEY LIVE IN
## stables

# HORSES CAN SLEEP STANDING UP!

It is possible due to a mechanism in their legs called the "stay apparatus", which allows them to lock their legs and keep them straight without much effort, enabling them to rest while standing.

# MATCH

Match the correct food for the horse by coloring.

Did you know?

A colt is a young male horse, specifically one that is under four years old. It is the male equivalent of the term filly, which refers to a young female horse.

# HELP THE Horses
# TO CHOOSE THE CORRECT FOOD.

*Color it.*

**AVOCADO**

**LUCERNE**

**POTATO**

**SPINACH**

**CELERY**

**ONION**

**PEAR**

**MEAT**

Did you know?

Once the male horse reaches four years of age, he is no longer called a colt, but rather a stallion (if not castrated) or a gelding (if castrated).

# UNSCRAMBLE
### FIND OUT THE NAMES OF THE FOOD THAT

horses love to eat.

PPELA

MWTLAENRO

ERLUCN

RAEP

AHY

SSARG

Did you know?

Typically, a mare (female horse) gives birth to one foal at a time. Twins are very rare but can occur in horses,

Help the **horse** to find his favorite fruits.

Color the path.

Did you know?

A BABY HORSE is called
FOAL

# Help the *horse* to find his love.
Color the path.

Did you know?

Female horses over 4 years old, are
called mares.

# Help the *mare* to find her foal.

Color the path.

Did you know?

Horses have excellent memory: Horses can remember people, places, and other horses for many years. They use this memory to navigate their surroundings and avoid dangers.

# Did you know?

Horses communicate with their ears: A horse's ears are highly expressive and can show their mood. For example, forward ears indicate interest, while pinned-back ears show anger or irritation.

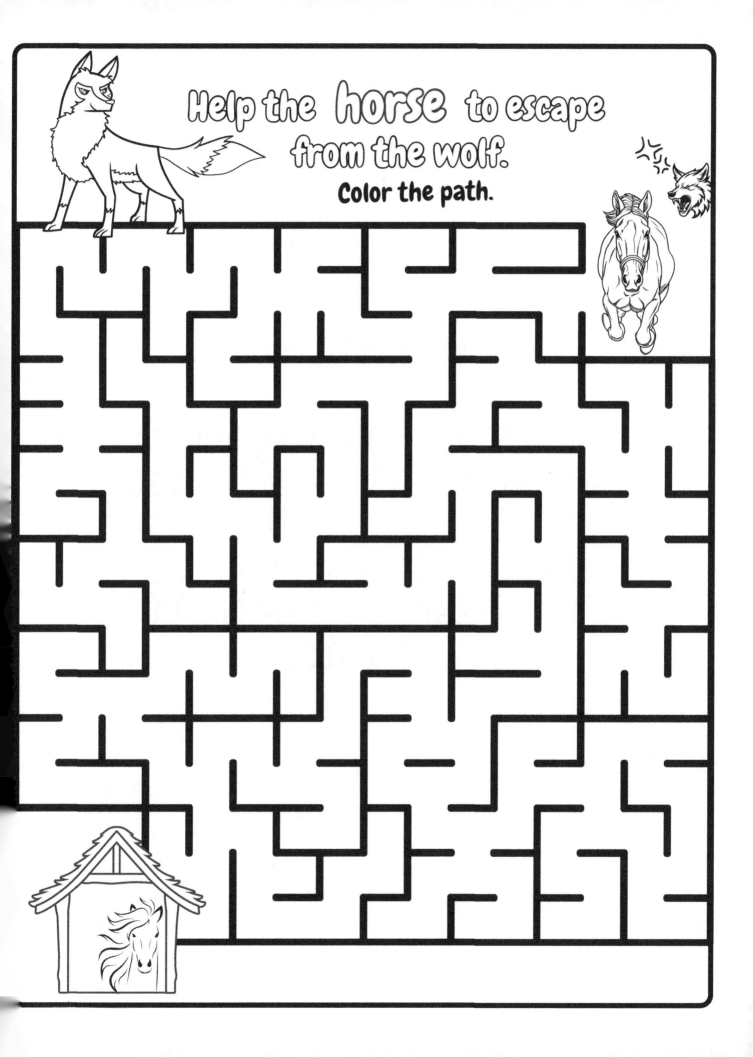

Help the **horse** to escape from the wolf.

Color the path.

Did you know?

A horse's heart can weigh up to 10 pounds: Horses have large, strong hearts that are essential for their endurance. Their hearts can beat up to 240 beats per minute during intense exercise.

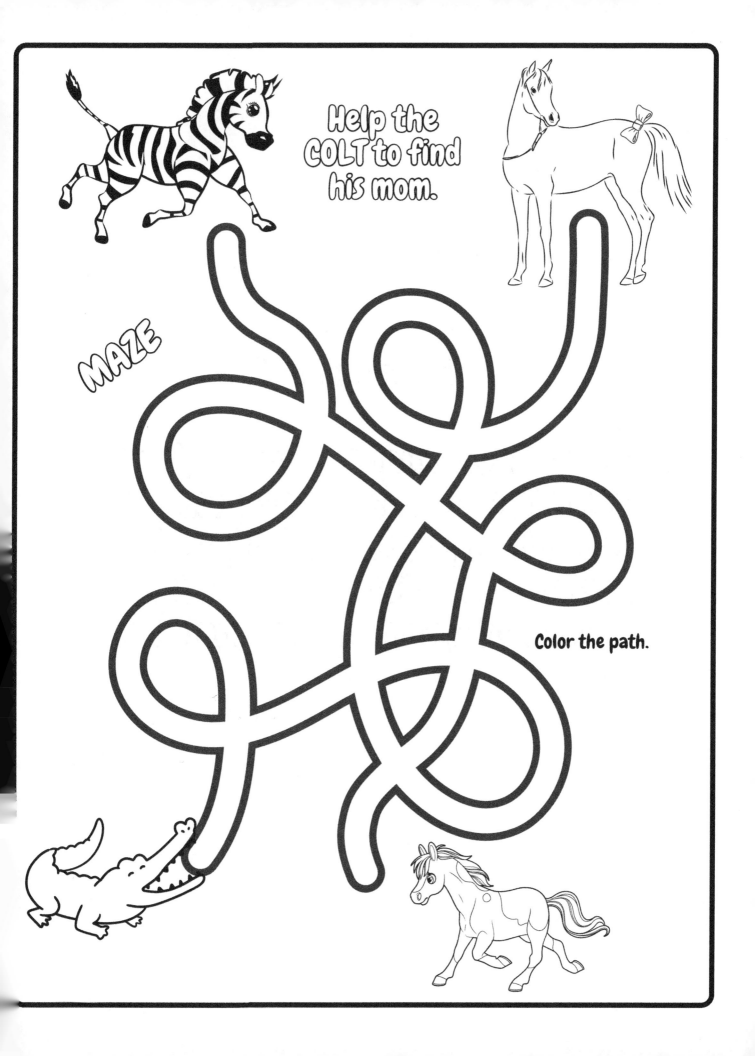

Help the
COLT to find
his mom.

MAZE

Color the path.

Did you know?

Horses have unique hooves: A horse's hoof is like a human fingerprint—each horse's hoof pattern is unique. Hooves are also incredibly strong and grow constantly throughout their life

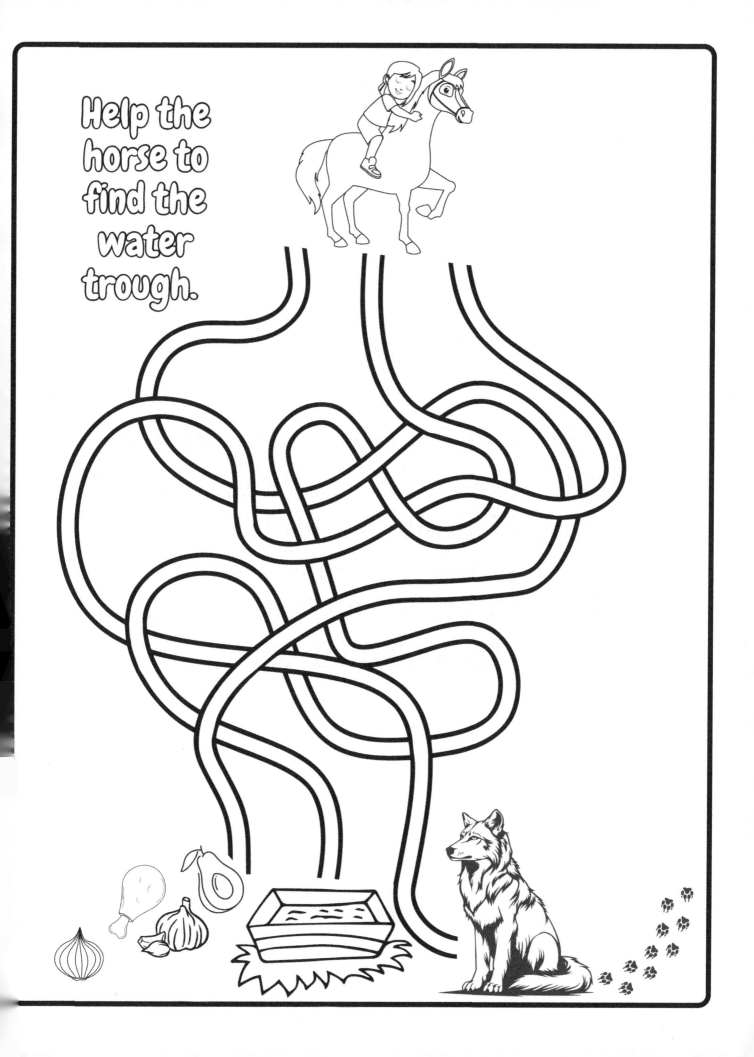

Help the horse to find the water trough.

Did you know?

Hooves are the hard, protective coverings on a horse's feet, similar to fingernails in humans. They allow horses to walk, run, and support their weight. Hooves grow continuously and need regular care.

# NAME EACH HORSE WITH A
## cute name

Did you know?

Horses can run shortly after birth:
Foals are born with the instinct to
stand and run within a few hours of
birth to avoid predators. This survival
trait is crucial for their safety in the
wild.

Did you know?

Their digestive system is designed for grazing, and they can spend up to 16 hours a day eating to support their energy needs.

# Find the two different rocking horses.

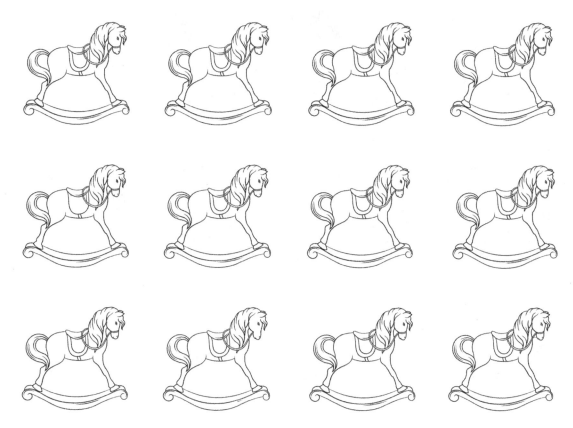

# Find the five differences .

# Find the two different foals.

# Find the five differences.

# Quiz

Color the correct answer.

How many teeth do horses can have?

44    12    20

How many foals can be born at once?

4    8    2

Where are they from?

Africa    Asia    North America

Thank you for your preference!!

# This book was designed by

## María Yehudí Hernández Bonilla

# In collaboration with

## Teacher Liliana Bonilla

# Find our books on

## amazon

Made in the USA
Las Vegas, NV
17 December 2024

14560652R00057